# Road

## Roadside America
## From Custard's Last Stand to the Wigwam Restaurant

Richard Longstreth

# Trip

Universe

*For Cinda,*
*My wife and companion on many of these forays during the 1970s*
*and during the decades that have followed*

First published in the United States of America in 2015
by UNIVERSE PUBLISHING
A Division of
Rizzoli International Publications, Inc.
300 Park Avenue South, New York, NY 10010
www.rizzoliusa.com

ISBN-13: 978-0-7893-2761-1
Library of Congress Control Number: 2014952567
© 2015 Universe Publications, Inc.
Text and Photography © 2015 Richard Longstreth

Designed by Douglas Curran

Distributed to the U. S. Trade by Random House, New York
Printed and bound in China
2015 2016 2017 2018 2019 / 10 9 8 7 6 5 4 3 2 1

Page 1: *Intersection of U.S. routes 15 and 250, Zion's Crossroads, Virginia (February 1971)*
Page 2–3: *Merle's Drive-In, Visalia, California (October 1974)*
Page 4–5: *U.S. Route 101, South of San Francisco, California (May 1972)*
Page 6–7: *Dreamland, U.S. Route 60, Kenova, West Virginia (July 1972)*
Pages 10–11: *Greenland Lodge Cabins, U.S. Route 30, western Pennsylvania (February 1971)*

# Contents

# Roadside Observations,
# An Introduction

THE REASON I BEGAN TAKING photographs of vernacular commercial buildings along American roadsides in the late 1960s is simple: they interested me. Why they interested me is a more elusive matter. I knew of no one who was doing similar work or even had a similar interest. I was then unaware of the writings of J. B. Jackson, a maverick essayist who played a key role in framing the concept of cultural landscape and who later became a good friend. Nor did I know of the photographs taken by Walker Evans and others employed by the Farm Security Administration to document ordinary life in the United States during the Depression. (In 1971 a friend who accompanied me on several of my forays mentioned Evans, whose images were starting to attract attention as art.) Nor did I know of contemporary painters such as Richard Estes, John Bader, or Ed Ruscha who turned to the commercial vernacular as a source of artistic exploration. (I did discover Ruscha's photographic work by 1972 through the little books he had issued, which were for sale at the art museum at the University of California, Berkeley, several of which I purchased at what then seemed a hefty price.)

Having spent four years as an undergraduate at the University of Pennsylvania (1964–68), I was familiar with the work of Robert Venturi and his associates (the office was then called Venturi & Rauch). I was an avid admirer of that firm's work, and had visited all of its realized buildings during the course of preparing a guide to architecture in Philadelphia and its environs, which I began as an independent study project during my final semester. I had read *Complexity and Contradiction in Architecture* shortly after it was issued in 1966 and became no less engrossed in a piece that Venturi and Denise Scott Brown co-authored for *Architectural Forum*: "A Significance for A&P Parking Lots or Learning from Las Vegas," which appeared in the spring of 1968.

Prior to that time, my interest in architecture (I thought I wanted to be an architect) and in architectural history (which I loved) focused on, for lack of a better term, the realm of high art. That interest deviated somewhat from what was then the norm in that it extended beyond the canon of modern architecture to encompass eclecticism of the nineteenth and early twentieth centuries. The work of McKim, Mead & White and Charles Adams Platt interested me as much as did that of Frank Lloyd Wright and Le Corbusier. My perspective was greatly enhanced by outlooks of two art history professors under whom I had the good fortune to study: the late George B. Tatum and James F. O'Gorman, whose views were ecumenical. I was also influenced by the example of David Gebhard, whose outlook toward architecture was even more embracing. His scholarship on California subjects was exploring realms that few, if any, of his colleagues nationwide considered worthy of serious study. Among his favorite pursuits were the Spanish Colonial Revival (his term) and Art Deco.

The Philadelphia guide, which was done under Jim O'Gorman's direction, gave me the opportunity to develop my still fledgling conception of what was significant in architecture more fully. Indeed, the project opened my eyes to a fact that for a long time since has seemed painfully obvious. A community's physical character is comprised of far more than a collection of individual "monuments."

PREVIOUS PAGES: *A & W Root Beer stand, U. S. Route 20, Alvorton, Ohio (October 1972)*
ABOVE: *Standard gasoline station, old U. S. Route 40, Lawrence, Kansas (April 1977)*

The urban context is essential, and the majority of that context is comprised of commonplace buildings. In Philadelphia, the most pervasive vernacular was (and is) the row house. Hundreds of thousands of speculative rows, from the eighteenth into the twentieth centuries, in many ways define what Philadelphia is as a city. By 1972, when I was completing my work on the guide, now as a co-author with the late Edward Teitelman under contract with MIT Press, I had traveled through every part of the city photographing hundreds of examples including semi-detached dwellings that emanated from the row house tradition and that had been built as recently as the pervious decade. My probes further stimulated an interest in postwar tract houses of the freestanding variety, most especially with Levittown, Pennsylvania, the maturing landscape of which seemed to contradict all the negative attributes propagated by sociologists, architecture critics, and others who had damned the phenomenon since it was new. It was, perhaps, not so great an intellectual leap of faith from ordinary houses to ordinary commercial buildings anchored to the nation's highways.

Circumstances facilitated the latter quest. Upon graduation, I received a commission in the U. S. Navy and soon drove from the East Coast to San Diego. Along the way, I made a point of visiting Las Vegas, which before Venturi and Scott Brown's article I had always considered flashy detritus. The experience proved worthwhile, but far from revelatory. What did change things was being in southern California over the next year-and-a-half (or at least that portion when my ship was in port). It was not my first time in the region. During the summer months of 1966, I had worked in Los Angeles, spending all my spare time visiting some of the extraordinary Arts-and-Crafts and Modern architecture that exists in the region. Yet three years later, many free hours were spent looking at gas stations and other automobile-related buildings, several of which are included in this volume.

In January 1970, I drove across country again to my second tour of duty, in Washington, D. C., attempting to record many roadside establishments along the way. During the next sixteen months, off-duty hours were spent driving to Philadelphia to continue working on the guide, taking a number of alternative routes in both directions. I also made additional trips expressly for the purpose of photographing things along the road. U. S. Route 1 between Massachusetts and southern Virginia, U. S. Route 40 between Atlantic City and Indianapolis, U. S. 30 in Pennsylvania, U. S. 301 in Maryland and Virginia, and countless of other roads in the Northeast as well as portions of the upper Midwest and South were traversed, yielding a stunning array of examples.

Devoting so much time (and money for gasoline, food, and color and black-and-white film) was done, to a degree, out of a sense of urgency. The interstate highway system was in its final stages of construction. The need for so many motorist services along the older, unlimited-access roads was quickly dissipating. Soon many of these places would be abandoned (a number already were), demolished, or altered for new functions. Highway-related commercial development had been ephemeral in nature from the start, but now the landscape of a whole era would likely vanish in short order.

After my term of active duty was concluded and I got married, my wife and I drove west again, this time to Berkeley, where I entered the new Ph.D. program in architectural history at the University of California's College of Environmental Design. Road trips throughout the West Coast and on several cross-country journeys over the next four years (1971–75) were followed by a move to work for the Rhode Island Historical Preservation Commission in Providence and yet another move to Manhattan, Kansas, in 1976, to begin my first teaching position in the state university's College of Architecture and Design. One more trip to San Francisco and one or two drives annually to the East, coupled with frequent explorations of Kansas and contiguous portions of the central United States, occurred before the decade's end. I never kept track of the distances, but can roughly estimate that, between January 1970 and December 1979, some 60,000 miles were covered, traversing all but a handful of states, as, all the while, I scouted for things along the road.

None of this effort had any immediate, concrete benefit to my career. Photography was not coupled with research leading to scholarly articles, a book, or even an exhibition that would have helped professionally. I did include some examples in the Philadelphia guide (many of which got cut when the geographic boundaries were narrowed to the city itself) and in the published survey I did for the Preservation Commission. By the time I was teaching in Kansas, I incorporated some of my findings into classes and began to lecture in other places on aspects of the subject to introduce people to what was still an unorthodox as well as new realm of inquiry. I did embrace Brinck Jackson's much earlier admonition to critics that the roadside landscape deserved serious study, if for no other reason than it was such a ubiquitous phenomenon nationwide. Yet launching one's scholarly career on exploring that phenomenon during the mid-1970s would have elicited more derision than interest among academics. Even more important, I was fully engrossed in researching aspects of eclecticism in the U. S. in the late nineteenth and early twentieth centuries, using the San Francisco Bay Area as a case study. Not until my dissertation, and the book that followed, were completed in 1983 did I have the urge to turn my sights elsewhere. That shift began in the mid-1980s, by which time I was teaching at George Washington University, and it was concentrated on twentieth-century retail development. My now longstanding interest in the roadside served me well, but the time of frequent road trips was over. I still enjoy driving long distances and still stop to record vestiges of an earlier era, but most of the things that abounded forty years ago have gone.

···

As a historian of the built environment, my primary concern in photographing the roadside landscape was documentary—to provide a long-term record of places that would soon disappear. The highway is a subject that has attracted photographers since at least the early 1930s, but I knew of no one who was addressing this subject at the outset of my efforts or who was dedicating so much time

*Bunyon's Hot Dogs, 6150 Ogden Street, Chicago, Illinois (February 1971)*
FOLLOWING PAGES: *Ship Hotel, 1928, 1931, U. S. Route 30, west of Bedford, Pennsylvania (February 1971)*

and covering so much geographic territory. My documentation was not a passive act—a snap shot without much thought as to composition or even the specific scope of information captured—though Ruscha's earlier images reveal how much meaning seemingly incidental images can possess. For me, photographing the environment was part of a process of discovery, of learning about things in ways other documentary evidence did not reveal fully, if at all. Photographs do not tell us everything—far from it—and photographs themselves are, of course, a form of editing—framing their subjects in ways that reflect the intentions of the photographer. My own approach was to let the subject speak for itself as much possible; that is, to avoid making it seem "better" or "worse" than it would appear with onsite viewing. At the same time, I wanted to make the images engaging and, since I was fascinated by the highway landscape, tried to convey at least some of my enthusiasm through these images. It was my hope that the commercial vernacular of the recent past would become the subject of scholarly study directed toward a better understanding of the profound ways in which the automobile has affected our world.

The images that follow are divided in to typological categories in part because much of my interest in such places centers on function, but also because so grouping them provides an instructive base for comparison whereby one can begin to see how multifaceted the constituent parts of the high-way landscape are. Well before I took my first photographs of this genre, that landscape was being de-rided for its monotony as well as its crassness. But my experience was just the opposite. Into the 1970s, an enormous variety could be found along the roadside, with multiple configurations of setting; with competing independent, franchise, and chain establishments; with varying approaches to design; and with ever-shifting views toward taste, marketing, and operation. The highway was home to a rich panoply of expression and experimentation—folk and corporate, sophisticated and naïve, exuberant and mundane, embellished and barebones—where change was continual, but also where survival was far more common than is generally thought. During the 1970s the highway remained a palimpsest of decades of development, with some components extending back to when highways were new and motoring a fresh experience.

An advantage to having a documentary record that is national in scope, rather than focusing on the work of a certain company or along a certain corridor, for example, is that a clearer sense of just how varied roadside architecture was, at least for its first half century of development. If we can discover most of what we need to know about the first century of skyscraper development by examining work in New York and Chicago, we must, conversely, look at the country as a whole to understand the myriad strains of roadside architecture. Among other things, the sampling of images contained in this book help reveal the spectrum of features that can characterize these places. To a degree, the images speak for themselves, at least in an evocative way. For each section, I offer a few observations that help place them in a larger context.

# Commercial Strips

ARTERIAL, OR STRIP, DEVELOPMENT catering to motorists has taken many forms since its inception in the 1920s. In numerous small towns, the strip did not exist as such; a clear divide existed between rural and more traditional community settings. Still service stations and other highway-oriented enterprises often formed a small cluster right at the edge, signaling the entry to a town as much as any more conventional landmark. In Paulsboro, New Jersey, the southern edge was defined by a creek and enunciated by a lift bridge, but is also clearly marked by signs for three gasoline stations (opposite page). In parts of the country where land was abundant, and inexpensive, these small clusters of automobile-oriented development could occupy much more space, as in Stanley Corners, South Dakota, where three service stations form a precinct of their own (following pages). Many older (pre–World War II) strips developed toward the periphery of cities were modest in size and appearance, housing small businesses and catering to a nearby residential population as much as, if not more than, transients, as seen in what was in the 1970s a rather rare intact example well to the south of downtown San Antonio (p. 26). A similar neighborhood orientation could be found in many towns. Irrespective of the community's size, buildings along such strips tended to be of a very elementary nature, without conspicuous features save, perhaps, signs. Small town centers could be transformed into strips once their main streets became major routes for motorized traffic, as with Metarie, Louisiana, where U. S. Route 61 served as the principal link between New Orleans and Baton Rouge (p. 30, top). Along the heaviest traveled interstate routes strip development catering to travelers could often be extensive by the mid-twentieth century, with a variety of services offered, becoming for the traveler a surrogate for the town center, where places for overnight accommodation and eating had previously clustered (pp. 28–29). By the mid-1960s major arterials running through sizable towns and cities alike could also spawn sizable retail and office projects that heralded the decentralization of key functions of those communities (p. 30, bottom). The intersection of primary overland routes had long spawned concentrations of highway-oriented businesses (pp. 32–33). The advent of the interstate highways led to instant strips at key interchanges, often demarked by signs of unusual elevation that could lure motorists from afar. In Fredericksburg, strip development along U. S. Route 1 initially concentrated near established parts of town, but the advent of Interstate Route 95 generated new and originally isolated strips anchored to its exits to the north and south (p. 31, bottom).

*U. S. Route 30, Paulsboro, New Jersey (May 1971)*
FOLLOWING PAGES: *Stanley Cafe and Gas, U. S. Route 14, Stanley Corners, South Dakota (October 1971)*

*Commercial strip, old U. S. Route 181, San Antonio, Texas (April 1971)*

*Commercial strip, Patterson, California (April 1975)*
FOLLOWING PAGES: *Commercial strip, U. S. Route 66, Shamrock, Texas (November 1972)*

*Commercial strip, Metarie Road (U.S. Route 61), Metarie, Louisiana (April 1974)*

*Commercial strip, Springfield, Missouri (August 1978)*

Commercial strip, U.S. Route 290, Fort Stockton, Texas (April 1974)

Commercial strip, U.S. Route 1 at I-95 intersection, Fredericksburg, Virginia (May 1970)

# Restaurants

Establishments purveying food, beverages, and sometimes entertainment along the highway could be found of almost every description. As motoring became a pastime in the early twentieth century, full-fledged restaurants—places long associated with the urban core—began to appear in number. Many were small, unpretentious places erected by their owners, often using imagery designed to catch the eye and suggest home cooking (opposite). Appearances were not always important. The Lettuce Inn in the agricultural center of Salinas, California, put stock in its name as well as, in all likelihood, the quality of its food and entertainment (following pages). Rose's Highway Inn was unusual in being well removed from concentrated settlement, lying on the outskirts of Tacoma, Washington, and depending upon a loyal following of area residents along with passing motorists (p. 40). While existing houses were sometimes enlarged and converted to accommodate their new function, Rose's appears to have been purpose-built. The proprietor may have had living quarters above, as seems to have been the case with Tucker's Steak House on the outskirts of New Orleans (p. 41). While many such restaurants sported domestic overtones (home cooking; family atmosphere), others utilized streamlined imagery of various sorts by the 1940s (p. 42). Modernizing in this vocabulary also provided a visually impactful way of enlarging a restaurant while masking its older parts. De Winne's Belgium Inn in San Antonio (p. 45, top) not only illustrates that practice, but also shows how what began as a neighborhood restaurant was transformed by imagery associated with the highway during the mid-twentieth century, when the highway was a style-setter in the popular mind, manifested both by automobiles and buildings serving them. Some owners relied more on signs than architectural development to attract their clientele—classic examples of what Robert Venturi characterized as the "decorated shed" (p. 44, bottom). On fewer occasions, configuring the establishment to suggest an enlarged or miniaturized object or thing of some sort—Venturi's "duck" (not shown) or in these cases ships and a wigwam—was used to strike a memorable image (pp. 44–45). While the great majority of these enterprises were locally owned and operated, Howard Johnson pioneered developing the highway restaurant as a regional chain, in the process creating a singular image and color scheme by the late 1930s that enhanced a sense of brand identity that fostered motorists to seek out his expanding network of units in the northeast (p. 43).

But the great majority of highway restaurants were smaller enterprises, specializing in fast food. Early on, these were humble establishments, often no more than open-air stands that were the product of more than one low-cost building campaign (pp. 46–48). By the late 1930s, chain companies began to emerge as potent forces in fast-food production. Located both along the highway and in town, they served hamburgers and a few other items with take-out or curb service far exceeding that available from their small counters. Type identity was achieved through veneers of porcelain enamel panels, while brand identity was enunciated by nods to traditional building features—crenellation for White Castle; a miniature house for Little Tavern—or by streamlining, where the corporate shingle formed an integral part of the design (pp. 49–51). Locally owned counterparts sought distinctiveness through images emblazoned on the front (p. 51) or with forms alluding to such novel objects as an accordion or, perhaps, a space ship (pp. 52–53).

PREVIOUS PAGES: *Commercial strip, state routes 99W and 99E, Junction City, Oregon (July 1974)*
THIS PAGE: *Square Cupboard Restaurant, U. S. Route 1, south of Fredericksburg, Virginia (May 1970)*
FOLLOWING PAGES: *Lettuce Inn, Salinas, California (March 1972)*

*Pioneer Take Out, Los Angeles, California (April 1974)*

Diners became a commonplace type of eatery in urban areas and along the highway alike by the 1930s, especially in the Northeast and occasionally in other parts of the country. Some were converted street, interurban, or long-distance railway cars adapted for the purpose, but with little change to their exteriors (p. 54). Others were conspicuously modified by their owners, probably to imbue them with a sense of modernity (p. 55, top). Many more were standard designs developed by manufacturers that specialized in this new building form (pp. 55, bottom, 56–59). Others give the appearance of being locally built, while attempting to follow a manufacturer's pattern. While maintaining a shoebox form loosely tied to railcars, diners took on a slicker, streamlined appearance and often sported more ambitious signs as well after World War II (p. 60). Boasting interiors that now always included booths, diners became ever more commodious as well as respectable even as the popularity of rail transit of all kinds was rapidly waning.

Drive-in restaurants quickly rose from being a novelty to a basic staple of the highway landscape by the 1950s. The type first proliferation in regions such as southern California, where a salubrious climate, a highly mobile population, and acres of boulevard frontage proved conducive to their development. More than the diner or even the hamburger stand, the drive-in was a mid-space object, designed to accommodate cars around most of its perimeter, and therefore generally depending upon a strong vertical element to identify the premises, as with a Wilshire Boulevard unit of Simon's, one of the type's pioneers (p. 64). After World War II, drive-ins became a poignant symbol of youthful exuberance and freedom in an increasingly affluent and permissive culture. Many establishments included indoor service that was welcome in cold and/or inclement weather and, by the mid-1950s, could impart a sense of drama through exaggerated forms. An alternative was to extend a canopy from the building that at least afforded some shelter to the car hops (p. 61, bottom).

Drive-ins were also popular for places specializing in root beer (A&W, in fact, was one of the pioneers of the drive-in concept) (p. 66, top) and diary products (p. 63), many examples of which mimed smaller or larger objects. Other exotic imagery could be marshaled to suggest the nature of the product dispensed (p. 62). By the mid-1950s, the most popular form for places selling frozen custard or root beer and, later, a somewhat larger menu was an embellished, enclosed "stand," with extensive glazing in front and often sporting a flared roof, bright color scheme, and eye-catching signs or objects (p. 67, top). Some enterprises experimented with broadening food choices—chicken and pastrami in the case of the Pioneer Take Out in Los Angeles (opposite). One establishment in Troy, New York, experimented with having two attached, but ostensibly separate operations provide in different offerings (p. 66, bottom).

The rise of franchise fast-food restaurants during the 1960s and 1970s entailed a series of brand images for buildings that became icons of the highway landscape. Kentucky Fried Chicken, for example, broke from the mold by combining elements associated with tradition (a pedimented doorway) incongruously combined with others more evocative of a carnival or even the Las Vegas strip (p. 67, bottom). While we tend to think of these establishments in terms of the largest and most enduring of companies, dozens of others have come and gone over the past half-century, many of them never extending beyond a limited region (p. 68). Irrespective of longevity, the architectural language of many of these establishments was cartoon-like, exaggerating and otherwise distorting elements in a manner traditionally associated with an amusement park. In other cases, familiar things were enlarged (p. 69) or miniaturized, reviving practices that were popular before World War II.

*Rose's Highway Inn, near Tacoma, Washington (July 1974)*

*Tucker's Steak House, Jefferson Highway (U. S. Route 61), Southport, Louisiana (April 1974)*

*State Garden Restaurant, U. S. Route 1, west of Clinton, Connecticut (April 1971)*

*Buckley's Restaurant, U. S. Route 40, Cumberland, Indiana (February 1971)*

*Former Flagship Restaurant, U. S. Route 11, west of Berwick, Pennsylvania (October 1971)*

*Howard Johnson's Restaurant, Baltimore Pike (U. S. Route 13), Media, Pennsylvania (May 1970)*

*Wigwam Restaurant, U.S. Route 301, Waldorf, Maryland (June 1971)*

*Baker's Steak House, State Route 5, Springfield, Pennsylvania (October 1972)*

DeWinne's Belgium Inn, 2619 Commerce Street, San Antonio, Texas (April 1974)

S. S. Flagship Furniture Clearance Center, formerly S.S. Flagship Restaurant, U. S. Route 46, Clifton, New Jersey (July 1971)

PREVIOUS PAGES: *Hamburger stand, Alexandria, Virginia (May 1970)*
ABOVE: *Blue Inn Restaurant and Grocery, U.S. Route 1, Fairfax County, Virginia (May 1970)*

*White Castle Hamburgers, Paramus, New Jersey (February 1970)*

BELOW: *Little Tavern Hamburgers, #14, M Street, N.W., Washington, D.C. (September 1970)*
CENTER: *White Tower Hamburgers, 14th and I streets, N.W., Washington, D.C. (September 1970)*
OPPOSITE PAGE: *Tommy's Hamburgers, Georgia Avenue and East-West Highway, Silver Spring, Maryland (May 1970)*

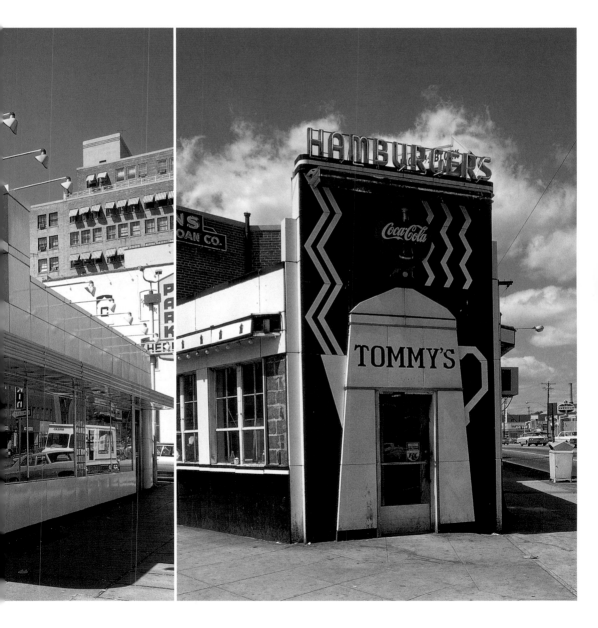

*Cully's Diner, Mason City, Iowa (October 1971)*

*Hamburger stand, U. S. Route 1, Elizabeth, New Jersey (February 1970)*

*Diner, U.S. Route 1, Virginia (May 1970)*

*Bing's Diner, Castroville, California (September 197?*

Pete & Pearl's Diner, Schenectady, New York (September 1970)

Wally's Diner, Schenectady, New York (September 1970)
FOLLOWING PAGES: O'Connor's Diner, Woonsocket, Rhode Island (April 1976); Empire Diner, Charleston, West Virginia (July 1972)

*Fernwood Diner, U. S. Route 13, Lansdowne, Pennsylvania (October 1970)*

*Maple Diner, U. S. Route 1, Elizabeth, New Jersey (February 1970)*

*u-Way Drive-In restaurant, Meyer Avenue and Trost Boulevard, Kansas City, Missouri (July 1972)*

*Al Green's Drive-In, U. S. Route 40, Indianapolis, Indiana (February 1971)*

*Beck's Frozen Custard, Washington, D. C. (May 1970)*

*The Milk Can, State Route 146, North Smithfield, Rhode Island (October 1975)*
FOLLOWING PAGES, LEFT TO RIGHT: *Former Simon's drive-in restaurant, 1936, Wilshire Boulevard, Los Angeles, California (1969);*
*Carvel Frozen Custard, Easton Road (State Route 611), Montgomery County, Pennsylvania (September 1970)*

*A & W Root Beer Stand, U. S. Route 20, Alvorton, Ohio (October 1972)*

*Neba Roast Beef Sandwiches and Mike's Submarines, Troy, New York (September 197*

*Custard's Last Stand, 1958, State Route 30, Long Lake, New York (July 1978)*

*Kentucky Fried Chicken, Anderson Avenue, Manhattan, Kansas (October 1978)*

*Former Deli-Land, U. S. Route 46, Clifton, New Jersey (July 1971)*

*Former Ox Hickory Fired Beef, U. S. Route 31, South Bend, Indiana (February 1971)*
FOLLOWING PAGES: *Oasis Drive-In, El Paso, Texas (April 1974)*

# Gasoline Stations

AS AUTOMOBILE USE PROLIFERATED during the interwar decades, gasoline stations became the most ubiquitous fixture of the highway landscape. Numerous early examples were built as service garages, in some cases for repair of horse-drawn vehicles, to which dispensing gasoline became an added feature. As with commercial stables, the building abutted the property line and now gas pumps lay close to the road (pp. 80–81). By the 1920s, garages were generally set back so that motorists could drive onto the premises to get gasoline (p. 82, top). The Saratoga Garage, situated on a major route extending north from Philadelphia also shows how such facilities could expand, with two service bays added to the original building (p. 83, top). Canopies, large and small, were founded on many examples to provide shelter from the elements for motorists and attendants (p. 82, bottom). The ad hoc nature of such enterprises took many forms irrespective of the scope of goods offered. A small filling station in Fredericksburg, Virginia, was enlarged with a roofed, but otherwise open-air, service bay (p. 83, bottom), while a service station in Shamrock, Texas, received an enormous, partially cantilevered canopy to protect its indoor spaces from the sun (pp. 84–85).

Gasoline as an offering could also be added to the goods sold in rural stores. L. H. Maloney's general store appears to have had few modifications save the gas pumps (p. 86). A complex of accretions in northern New Jersey augmented store sales not only with fuel but also with Ford parts (p. 86, top). Along U. S. Route 66, a nameless emporium included bull horns, presumably for a local trade, as well as gifts for tourists (following pages). A number of establishments appear to have been built to accommodate food and gas sales, especially in the vicinity of tourist destinations and in places were markets were scarce (pp. 88–89). This practice continued after World War II in some rural areas, well before the franchise convenience store became a common fixture.

While local entrepreneurs were responsible for a broad spectrum of gasoline outlets, many others were of standardized design developed by major oil companies. Prior to the 1930s, such places were often limited to gas and motor oil. A very early example in El Paso, probably designed for the Gulf Oil Company, is no more than an elaborate kiosk, with minimal enclosed space, around which several pumps once existed (p. 90, top). Small units were especially common in urban areas where land was costly. The Atlantic (Arco) filling station in Northeast Philadelphia is a typical example from the 1920s, with a utilitarian kiosk positioned at the rear corner to allow maximum space for cars (p. 90, bottom). Many stations had porte-cocheres to provide some shelter and also give the facility a more conspicuous presence (p. 90, top). Prefabricated steel designs, while more costly, speeded construction and were durable (pp. 92–93). They proliferated on the West Coast, but were rare in other parts of the country. A somewhat altered example in Oregon reveals a common practice of adding service function to these minimal buildings (p. 91, bottom). In many cases, particularly in the Southwest and southern California, service buildings were added to the property and differed from the standardized station design.

During the 1920s, especially, gasoline stations were frequently cast as a blight to the landscape. Oil companies and independent owners alike sought to mitigate such criticism by building more

*Sinclair service station, Broadway and 12th Street, Oklahoma City, Oklahoma (October 1972)*
FOLLOWING PAGES: *Bull Horn gasoline station and gift shop, U. S. Route 66, McLean, Texas (November 1972)*

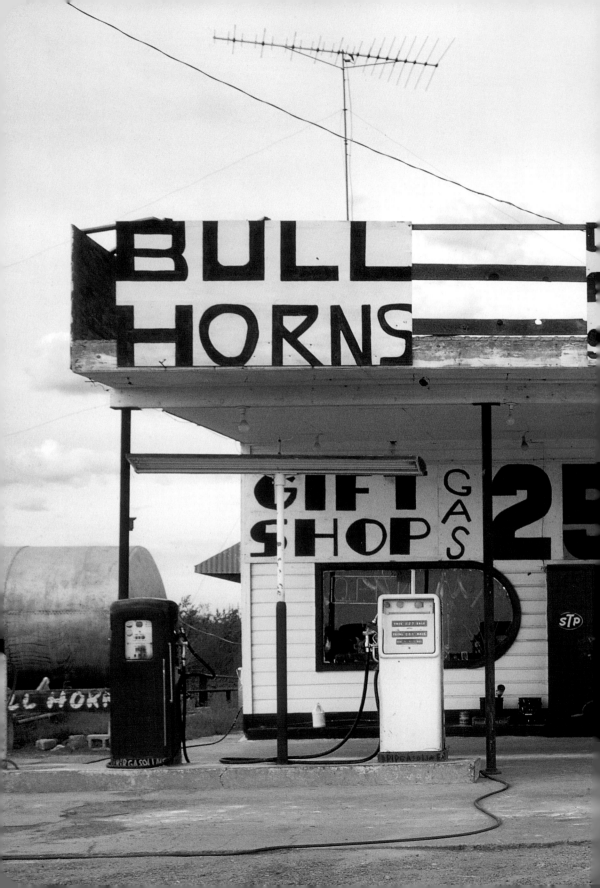

decorous units, of which the station built by the Standard Oil Company (later Esso) in Washington, D. C. is a telling example (p. 94). Standard Oil designed a series of exceptionally elaborate stations for metropolitan Boston, conceived in all likelihood to seduce the passing motorists as well as to placate civic concerns (p. 95). Occasionally a one-of-a-kind scheme would be built in a fashionable residential area (p. 79). While more the exception than the rule, historicizing imagery was often marshaled in such cases. Singular designs were developed when an owner wished to make a strong visual statement, perhaps as much to satisfy his ego as to attract customers (p. 76). These personalized facilities could be quite ambitious, as in South San Francisco, where a filling station is the frontispiece to a complex that contained a tiered apartment building, with what appears to have been a restaurant to one side (p. 96, top). In the small, north-central Kansas town of Glen Elder, a proud entrepreneur erected a stone service station with medievalizing overtones that surely cost more than was necessary given a limited market (p. 97, top). Similar ambitions seem to have inspired the storybook picturesqueness of a small service station near Liberty, Missouri, or a sizable complex that included a Plymouth dealership in northwestern Pennsylvania (p. 96, bottom, pp. 98–99). Historical allusions were more often minimal (and inexpensive), as with a vaguely Spanish station in western Kansas (p. 97). As with restaurants, gas stations could mimic familiar objects as a means of attracting attention, such as an iceberg, teepee, or oil can (pp. 14, 102). This practice continued into the mid-twentieth century, with cowboy gear inflated to giant proportions in Seattle (pp. 100–101). On occasion, too, an object itself could be appropriated for the enterprise, as with a de-commissioned World War II aircraft moved to western Oregon (pp. 104–105).

By the 1930s various strains of modernism were embraced by oil companies and independent dealers alike. Even minor manipulations of form following the conventions of Art Deco could turn a utilitarian box into a sculptural beacon (p. 103). The effect might be reserved, jazzy, or streamlined. Towers, popularized by the California world's fairs of 1915 and, especially by the Century of Progress Exposition of 1933, became a popular means of making a facility conspicuous to approaching drivers. One example in Oklahoma City combined an ornate, Spanish-inspired tower with an otherwise non-referential building (p. 73). More frequently, the tower was treated as an integral part of the composition, as seen in the ornate concrete filigree articulating the roofline of a service station-cafe complex in north Texas (p. 106, top) or the elegant simplicity of an all-concrete station near Yakima, Washington (p. 107, top). For a flagship station sited next to Kansas City's Union Station and Liberty Memorial Skelly Oil Company erected a sizable facility that was unusually monumental in its appearance, while capped with an enormous sign (p. 106, bottom).

Streamlined variations on Art Deco became popular by the late 1930s, when major oil companies set the style, often using designs where standardized components, many of them metal, could be assembled in various ways depending upon the site and the needed size of the outlet (pp. 108–109). Signs were generally treated as integral features of the design. Building, graphics, and color scheme were all marshaled to create bold impressions to foster an increased reliance on brand identity. Independent owner and small chain companies followed suit, with varying degrees of sophistication. Before World War II, Texaco pursued branding to the fullest extent, commissioning industrial designer Walter Dorwin Teague to design its stations, graphics, product containers, an even attendant uniforms. Teague's slick packaging in porcelain-enamel panels and glass set the standard for major oil company stations well into the 1950s, although the porte cochere was generally absent in units built after World War II (pp. 110–111). Signs and color schemes distinguished one company's operations from another more than form or architectural character. Even when an outlet was substantially larger than the norm, major oil companies sought a consistency in overall appearance.

Beginning in the 1920s major tire companies entered the lucrative market of purveying gasoline and automobile service, well before this practice became standard among oil producers. But unlike the compact service stations that the latter would build by the mid-1930s, tire manufacturers favored sizable complexes capable of handling many cars at one time. In cities, such facilities ranked among the largest and most conspicuous facilities related to the automobile (p. 114, top). The trend continued through the depression decade, when streamlining was marshaled to striking effect and into the post–World War II years as well. Occasionally, oil companies sought to compete with these service centers, but seldom, if ever, at the same scale (p. 115, top). By the late 1930s, other sizable facilities were built along the highway catering to truckers, where food and showers were an important part of the equation. In a number of towns, too, a gas station, extensive repair and parts facilities, and restaurant were combined, sometimes with dramatic effect (pp. 114, bottom, 115, bottom). At the opposite end of the equation were the modest outlets erected during the post–World War II years by companies that purchased surplus oil products and sold them at a discount. Frequently these stations were little more than embellished sheds—latter-day versions of the kiosks of the 1920s (p. 73). In some cases, however, the station also sold a limited array of food and beverages—a combination soon embraced by convenience store chains (p. 117).

*Texaco service station, Brentwood, California (July 1966)*

*Forestville Garage, Marlboro Pike, Prince George's County, Maryland (January 1971)*

*Garage and Phillips 66 gasoline station, Strong City, Kansas (October 1976)*

*Limerick Garage, Ridge Pike, Montgomery County, Pennsylvania (October 1970)*

*Former gasoline station and garage, Blue Rapids, Kansas (February 197*

*Sanatoga Garage, Ridge Pike, Montgomery County, Pennsylvania (October 1970)*

*Mobil gasoline station, Fredericksburg, Virginia (March 1970)*
FOLLOWING PAGES: *Shell service station, U. S. Route 66, Shamrock, Texas (November 1972)*

*L. H. Maloney gasoline station and general store, alt. U. S. Route 113, Magnolia, Delaware (August 1971)*

*Mobil gasoline station and general store, County Route 571, Ridgewood, New Jersey (August 1976)*
FOLLOWING PAGES: *Esso gasoline station and grocery store, U. S. Route 50, west of Ocean City, Maryland*

*Former Gulf (?) gasoline station, El Paso, Texas (April 1974)*

*Atlantic gasoline station, Frankford district, Philadelphia, Pennsylvania (August 197(*

*Texaco gasoline station, San Diego, California (June 1969)*

*Lance Labish Oil Company service station, State Route 99E, north of Salem, Oregon (July 1974)*
FOLLOWING PAGES: *Hancock gasoline station, Los Angeles, California (1969)*

*Humble (Esso) gasoline station, Pennsylvania Avenue and 26th Street, N. W., Washington, D. C. (August 1970)*

*Russo's Esso service station, Malden, Massachusetts (September 1972))*

*Rio Grande gasoline station and Babe's Tower, Bay Shore Road, South San Francisco, California (January 1972)*

*Former White Hall gasoline station, old U. S. Route 69, Glannaire, Missouri (July 197*

L. Norton service station, U. S. Route 24, Glen Elder, Kansas (March 1979)

Conoco service station, old U. S. Route 40, Grinnell, Kansas (October 1977)

FOLLOWING PAGES: Service station and Plymouth dealership, Brookville, Pennsylvania (October 1971)

PREVIOUS PAGES: *Hat n' Boots gasoline station, E. Marginal Way and Carson Street, Seattle, Washington (July 1974)*
ABOVE: *Gasoline station, U. S. Route 59, Ottawa, Kansas (May 1977)*

*Former Sinclair service station, U.S. Route 14, Wall, South Dakota (October 1971)*
FOLLOWING PAGES: *Bomber gasoline station, State Route 99E, Milwaukee, Oregon (July 1974)*

*Fina service station and Tower Cafe, U.S. Route 66, Shamrock, Texas (October 1972))*

*Skelly service station, Kansas City, Missouri (July 1972)*

*andard gasoline station, U. S. Route 12, Naches, Washington (July 1974*

*Union 76 service station, Tucson, Arizona (February 1970)*

*Standard service station, San Diego, California (July 1969)*

*Richfield service station, University Avenue, San Diego, California (July 1969)*

*Amoco service station, Duke Street, Alexandria, Virginia (December 1970)*

*Former Tydal service station, U. S. Route 40, Maryland (July 1970)*
FOLLOWING PAGES: *Whiting Brothers service station, U. S. Route 66, Holbrook, Arizona (November 1972)*

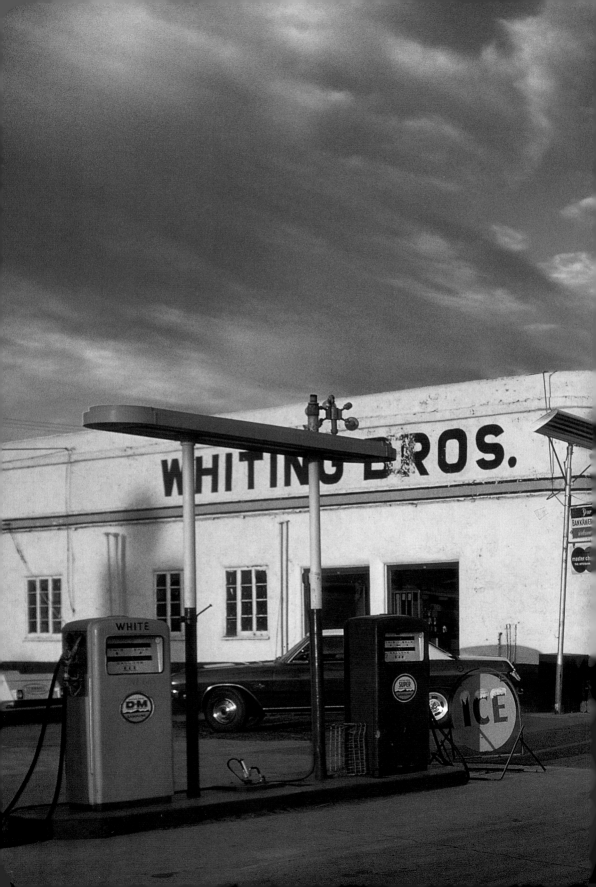

*Firestone service center, Texas and Octavia streets, El Paso, Texas (April 1974)*

*Airline Motors service station and restaurant, U.S. 61, LaPlace, Louisiana (April 197*

*Esso service station, Baltimore, Maryland (May 1971)*

*Former service station and restaurant, old U. S. Route 40, Russell, Kansas (October 1977)*

*Wake Up gasoline station, U. S. Route 36, Indianapolis, Indiana (February 1971)*

*Scot gasoline station, Annapolis, Maryland (April 1970)*
FOLLOWING PAGES: *Service station and garage, U. S. Route 101, Port Angeles, Washington (July 1971)*

# Motels

THE SURGE IN LONG-DISTANCE travel by motorists during the 1920s failed to spawn roadside hotels. Instead, scores of multi-story hotels catering to drivers were constructed in core of towns and cities across the country. There was a scattering of exceptions, none of which were more idiosyncratic the Ship Hotel on U. S. 30 in Alleghenies of western Pennsylvania (pp. 20–21). While accommodations were hardly luxurious, the exotic appeal of sleeping in a marooned "ship" with sweeping views of the landscape proved sufficient to keep the establishment running for some five decades. But if they were not partial to a hotel downtown, most travelers opted for a new alternative, the motel, by virtue of the privacy and convenience it afforded, the informality it allowed, and the economy it enabled. By 1940s, American highways gave life to thousands of motels, the great majority of them containing a dozen units or less and almost all of them locally owned.

Like the highway restaurant, the motel proved fertile ground for people who were entre-preneurial and lived along well-traveled routes. It was not unusual for farmers to augment their incomes by adding "cottages" or "cabins" for travelers (opposite). Often the process occurred incrementally, as capital permitted. Building a restaurant added or adjacent to the owner's house was also a widespread practice aimed at attracting a larger audience (p. 122). Guest quarters were typically in detached cabins that were very small by later standards and elementary in nature (124–125). In some cases, however, owners invested heavily in their enterprises, with sizable units that were decidedly domestic in char-acter (p. 127). A number of these complexes boasted sheltered bays in between each unit for guests' cars at a time when many vehicles had only canvas tops (p. 126). Even though motels of the interwar decades were often developed in stages, the ensemble was usually organized in an orderly fashion. Probably the most common arrangement was as a row running at right angles to the road or some-times parallel to it. For larger establishments, forming a court, with two ranges facing one another and, perhaps, a third, joining range at the far end, with the office placed as a centerpiece at the front, became a widespread pattern (p. 130).

Geographical variations were not pronounced in early motels, but a few such patterns did exist. In California, for example, a number of examples were configured in a manner similar to small apartment complexes in that region, with one- and two-story buildings clustered around a central court that, for motels, accommodated cars instead of a landscaped common space (pp. 134–135). The pioneering chain of Alamo Plaza Motor Hotels, begun in the 1930s in Texas and extending to the Southeast, had portals leading to a large central court, off of which lay building clusters facing sec-ondary courts—a configuration inspired by an assortment of regional precedents (p. 136, top). Well before then, many motels in the Southwest possessed imagery suggestive of the region's Spanish—or, in New Mexico, its pueblo Indian—heritage (pp. 138–139)—allusions for which the South and the Northeast had few counterparts until after World War II. Built during the mid-1930s, the Matador Motel in Northern California broke from the fold in the sophistication with which Spanish-inspired elements were used (p. 137, top). It was no less unusual in its size and in its row configuration, with

*Locust Grove Cottages, State Route 60, Washington County, Indiana (January 1978)*

*National Trail Cabins and Restaurant, U. S. Route 40, Ohio (February 1971)*
FOLLOWING PAGES: *Former Americana Motel, U. S. Route 1, south of Baltimore, Maryland (April 1971)*

units sheltered by arcades and porches. Unlike most motels of the era, it was probably designed by an architect.

The design resolution manifested in the Matador occurred at a time of numerous, less decisive experiments in attempts to break from the cabin mold. The Tres Pinos Inn, in a central California valley, manifests the transition, with twin cabins joined by decorative arches—all appended to the arcuated restaurant and office (pp. 144–145). An unnamed Maryland motel catering to African Americans at a time when most hostelries excluded them had alternating "cabins" and smaller units, the latter perhaps added, to form a syncopated rhythm (p. 137, bottom). Constructing units in a row brought economies in construction and maintenance, and thus appealed to many entrepreneurs. The Minan-A1 Court on U. S. Route 1, just north of Richmond or Porter's Motel in south-central Nebraska were typical of many row designs by the decade's end (p. 142). The boxy character of these places was sometimes relieved by such low-cost embellishments as entry shelters and decorative parapets (p. 143). Some enterprises were less bare bones, using masonry construction, raised terrace connecting entries, and an eye-catching design for the office, for example, to convey the appearance of a "better" facility (p. 146).

The post–World War II era brought a new boom in motel construction. For at least a dozen years independently owned businesses remained dominant in the trade. These hostelries tended to include a greater number of units, with larger and more commodious rooms. Row configurations prevailed, and many exteriors possessed a low-key, vaguely streamlined character (p. 147). By the mid-1950s, new amenities such as air conditioning and television, as well as other suggestions of luxury were conspicuously displayed (p. 149). Many motels were well set back from the highway to mitigate noise and enhance privacy, with sweeping expanses of lawn as well as ornamental landscaping contributing to a sense of prestige (p. 150). Some facilities boasted gardens (p. 151, top) or, with increasing frequency, a swimming pool. The Jay Hawk Motel outside Topeka, Kansas, represents the culmination of independently owned roadside accommodations (p. 151, bottom). Constructed by that city's major hotel company to take advantage of a newly constructed bypass highway, the establishment was a large, sprawling affair, with dozens of units set amid acres of lawn and anchored to a capacious restaurant. The design exuded modernity, while nodding to tradition with a gable roof and a cupola rendered in a "colonial" vein popularized by Howard Johnson (who was by then entering the motel business). While representing a major investment, the motel was soon marooned by the alignment of the new Interstate Route 70 close to downtown and well to the south of the Jay Hawk's site.

*Moon Motel, Wichita, Kansas (September 1976)*

*Melinda Motel, U. S. Route 50, Springfield, Missouri (August 1978)*
FOLLOWING PAGES: *Colony Motel, U. S. Route 1, Beltsville, Maryland (April 1971)*

*Blue Bird Court, U. S. Route 90, San Antonio, Texas (April 1971)*

*Golden Gate Motel, San Pablo Avenue (State Route 17), El Cerrito, California (January 1972)*
FOLLOWING PAGES: *Grande Motel, U.S. Route 87, Amarillo, Texas (November 1972);*
*Monte Vista Motel, U.S. Route 66, Duarte, California (September 1974)*

GRANDE COURT
LOOK
2 PERSONS $4.00
ALSO FAMILY RATES
HOT WATER
SHOWER
Air Conditioned

*Alamo Plaza Motor Hotel, 1948, 4343 Old Spanish Trail, Houston, Texas (April 1974)*

*Anderson Motel, State Route 99, Merced, California (September 1974)*

*Matador Motel, ca. 1935, W. Tenth Avenue (State Route 99), Chico, California (July 1974)*

*Cabins—"Colored," U. S. Route 1, south of Baltimore, Maryland (April 1971)*

FOLLOWING PAGES: *Geronimo Motor Lodge, Tucson, Arizona (April 1974)*

PREVIOUS PAGES: *La Mesa Motel, U. S. Route 66, Albuquerque, New Mexico (November 1972)*
ABOVE: *Former Porter's Motel, U. S. Route 30, Chappell, Nebraska (August 1975)*

*Motel, State Route 309, south of Allentown, Pennsylvania (October 1971)*
FOLLOWING PAGES: *Tres Pinos Inn, State Route 25, Tres Pinos, California (May 1975)*

*Motel, Fredericksburg, Virginia (May 1970)*

*Motel, U. S. Route 40, north of Baltimore, Maryland (July 1970)*

*Skyline Motel, U. S. Route 40, Columbus, Ohio (February 1971)*

*Motel Edgewood, U.S. Route 40, Edgewood, Maryland (July 1970)*

*Green Acres Motel, U. S. Route 40, north of Baltimore, Maryland (July 1970)*

*Cadillac Motel, U. S. Route 1, Virginia (May 1970)*

West End Gardens Motel, U.S. Route 40, Maryland (July 1970)

Jay Hawk Motel, old U.S. Route 40, North Topeka, Kansas (June 1977)
FOLLOWING PAGES: Alamo Motel, U.S. Route 50, west of Ocean City, Maryland (August 1970)

# Stores

FEW RETAIL FACILITIES WERE more affected by the automobile than food stores, of which the supermarket became the most ubiquitous and long-lasting product. The supermarket concept entailed purveying all kinds of food and kitchen-related merchandise under one roof in a single, integrated operation, where customers served themselves to most products and paid for them in one place rather than at multiple vendor stands. The system was predicated on volume sales, enabling low prices. Only with cars, of course, could customers make volume purchases and only with cars could they conveniently access these giant emporia that were fewer in number and thus tended to lie further afield than the abundant array of small, neighborhood food outlets that depended upon pedestrian trade. Ralphs Grocery Company in Los Angeles repeatedly set national standards during the supermarket's inceptive period between the late 1920s and early 1940s. A Beverly Hills unit of 1937, oriented as much to its huge parking lot as to the street, reveals how the company invested heavily in appearances as well as in the utilitarian necessities of its operations, with an exuberant design that exuded glamour as well as modernity (opposite). Few other companies were as venturous. Irrespective of exterior panache, most early supermarkets were firmly anchored to the street, leaving motorists to fend for themselves in securing a space for their cars (following pages). Some vendors were even more conservative. Pulmo's Food Mart in a northern California agricultural center, gives evidence of originally having five small-scale concessionaires in adjacent spaces, each with its own entrance (p. 158). Off-street parking was provided, but only for a few cars in a strip fronting the premises. By mid-century, however, many West Coast food purveyors followed Ralphs's lead, sometimes even imitating that company's store designs (pp. 160–161). Houston, another important center for the supermarket's early development, had its own varieties of large, conspicuous buildings oriented entirely to the parking lot (p. 163). The supermarket became a national phenomenon after World War II, with examples constructed in many towns as well as in metropolitan centers (pp. 164–165).

Aside from New York, the supermarket was a rare exception in most East Coast cities until the postwar years. Washington, D. C.–based Giant Stores was one of the pioneers, and by the early 1950s it produced an array of bold modernist designs (p. 166, left). In Philadelphia, Food Fair was the industry leader, its huge stores enunciated by multi-story pylons (pp. 166–167). A competitor, Acme Markets, developed a series of signature vertical signs atop expansive, transparent fronts (p. 168). In San Francisco, Lucky markets set the postwar standard in their design (p. 169). The much larger San Francisco–based Safeway chain proved more reluctant to embrace the supermarket concept fully. Not until the late 1950s did it construct units comparable to those of Ralphs or Food Fair. By then, new units around the company's home region possessed exuberant forms and polychromatic exterior color schemes that rendered them among the region's most conspicuous highway landmarks (pp. 170–173). Elsewhere, Safeway stores remained more conservative in their appearance (p. 174). Nationwide, many regional chains experimented with designs that would distinguish their

*Ralphs Grocery Company store, 1937, 9331 Wilshire Boulevard, Beverly Hills, California (1969)*
FOLLOWING PAGES: *Roman Foods Market, Wilshire Boulevard, Los Angeles, California (May 1972)*

*Plumo's Food Mart, Yuba City, California (April 1973)*
FOLLOWING PAGES: *New Island Market, Alameda, California (July 1973)*

operations in the public mind; few building types were more aggressively modernist in the postwar era (p. 175).

Drug store companies were among the first to follow the supermarket's lead in offering a great spectrum of merchandise at low prices through self-service. As early as 1934, a unit of Katz drug stores in Kansas City erected a lavish emporium that rivaled the most ambitious southern California supermarkets (pp. 176–177). After World War II, chain variety stores began to make the switch, while they also expanded the scope of their businesses to become more competitive with downtown department stores. A three-story C. G. Murphy Company unit that was the largest retail emporium in Clarendon, Arlington County, Virginia's primary business center, exemplified the trend (p. 178). Clarendon boomed in the late 1940s and early 1950s, but was soon thereafter eclipsed by the even faster growth of the shopping center.

Washington, D. C., became a key proving ground for the shopping center concept—a group of stores selected to complement one another, forming an integrated business developed, owned and managed by a single party—during the depression decade. After a successful 1930 prototype that fused the concept with a set-back configuration allowing a generous parking area at the property's front, numerous examples were erected in the region prior to World War II (p. 179). These were modest affairs generally containing fewer than twenty stores—all of them purveying everyday goods and services. Many more were constructed after the war's end to serve burgeoning residential development around the city. While some, such as the Washington and Lee Shopping Center in Arlington had more conservative layouts, with storefront abutting the sidewalk and parking across the street (p. 180, top) or to the building's rear, an ever-larger front-end parking area became the norm by the mid-1950s. The postwar shopping center boom was, of course, a national phenomenon, with examples proliferating throughout metropolitan suburbs and in many towns alike (pp. 180, bottom, 181, top). During this period, too, hundreds of these complexes were built with a larger number of stores and included major chain supermarket and variety store outlets serving as their business anchors (p. 181, bottom). An increase in building size and an ever greater rise in acreage dedicated to parking led to a reliance on multi-storied, freestanding signs at the property's edge to give motorists a sense of shopping center's tenant complexion (p. 183). By the late 1950s, the regional shopping center, with upwards of sixty or more outlets and a downtown department store branch as the anchor became a widespread phenomenon. By that time, too, the preferred configuration for these sprawling competitors with the city center was around a mall, with an encircling car lot, so that customers could walk freely from store to store without the hazards of traffic. The Wampanog Mall in Rhode Island was a modest variation on this patter, with a low-price chain oriented to the parking area as the anchor (p. 182). If the most conspicuous trend was toward bigness, many other shopping centers were erected at a more modest scale, with ten or fewer stores serving a local trade.

Some major retailers resisted participating in shopping center development in the belief that their businesses were sufficiently larger and well known to operate independently. Since the mid-1920s Sears, Roebuck had grown to become one of the nation's largest retailers with department stores situated apart from shopping districts of any size. Sears continued these lone-wolf emporia, some with rooftop parking decks to accommodate patrons, well into the 1950s (p. 184). Other chain department stores continued this stand-alone siting pattern for another decade (p. 185).

The sale of motor vehicles was a less mercurial trade. Into the third quarter of the twentieth century, it was not that unusual to find car dealers, especially in towns, that still utilized their plants from pre-Depression years (p. 186–187). But in larger communities, many dealerships moved after World War II from in-town locations to ones along major routes further afield where ample space could be procured for a horizontally organized building and off-street parking (p. 188, top). Automobile manufacturers encouraged dealers to erect facilities that bespoke the style-conscious modernity of automobile designs that became particularly strong by the mid-1950s. Some dealers invested extravagantly in showrooms that were beacons of commerce (p. 188, bottom). Building strikingly modern quarters occurred in many smaller communities as well (pp. 190–191). By contrast, used car lots, whether operated by a major car dealer or an independent businessman, generally had small, unassuming offices, relying on an extensive use of signs to attract attention (p. 189, top). Large-scale truck and farm equipment dealers had little incentive to construct eye-popping facilities. Many examples, however, embody the value of efficiency, economy, and newness in the machines they harbored (p. 189, bottom).

*Giant supermarket, Old Spanish Trail and Telephone Road, Houston, Texas (April 1974)*
FOLLOWING PAGES: *Dillon's Market, St. John's, Kansas (November 1977)*

BELOW: *Giant supermarket, 1950–51, First and St. Asaph streets, off U. S. Route 1, Alexandria, Virginia (September 1970)*
CENTER: *Food Fair supermarket, 5300 block York Boulevard, Baltimore, Maryland (May 1971)*
OPPOSITE PAGE: *Pantry Pride (formerly Food Fair) supermarket, Elkins Park, Pennsylvania (September 1970)*

*Acme supermarket, Ingleside Shopping Center, U. S. Route 40, Catonsville, Maryland (May 1971)*
OPPOSITE PAGE: *Lucky supermarket, State Route 77, San Leandro, California (May 1972)*
FOLLOWING PAGES: *Safeway supermarket, Vallejo, California (January 1972)*

PREVIOUS PAGES: *Safeway supermarket, Walnut Creek, California (March 1973)*
ABOVE: *Safeway supermarket, Price, Utah (July 1972)*

*Skagg's Thrifty City, Springfield, Missouri (August 1978)*
FOLLOWING PAGES: *Katz drug store, 1934, 3954 Main Street, Kansas City, Missouri (July 1972)*

OPPOSITE PAGE: *Murphy's variety store, 1948–49, Wilson Boulevard, Arlington, Virginia (June 1971)*
ABOVE: *Greenway Shopping Center, 1940–41, 3525–54 E. Capitol Street, N. E., Washington, D. C. (1971)*

*Washington and Lee Shopping Center, Arlington, Virginia (December 1970)*

*Vern's Shopping Center, Telegraph Avenue, Oakland, California (July 197_*

*Food City and shopping center, Napa, California (February 1974)*

*Lansdowne Shopping Center, U. S. Route 13, Lansdowne, Pennsylvania (October 1972)*

*Wampanoag Mall, 1967–69, 1925 Pawtucket Avenue, East Providence, Rhode Island (October 1975)*
OPPOSITE PAGE: *Great Eastern Shopping Center, Marlboro Pike, Prince George's County, Maryland (January 1971)*

*Sears Roebuck department store, 1946–47, Geary Boulevard and Masonic Avenue, San Francisco, California (January 1972)*

*Grant's department store, Santa Clara, California (January 1972)*
FOLLOWING PAGES: *Former Studebaker sales and service building, Pleasantville, New Jersey (June 1972)*

*Martin Chevrolet sales and service building, Richmond, Virginia (January 1978)*

*Former Buick sales and service building, St. Helens and 6th Avenue, Tacoma, Washington (July 197...*

*ed Jones Ford used car lot, Tulsa, Oklahoma (November 1978)*

*International Harvester sales and service building, Dallas, Texas (November 1978)*
FOLLOWING PAGES: *Arena Oldsmobile sales and service building, Black Horse Pike, New Jersey (September 1970)*

# Theaters and Other Places
# of Entertainment

DURING THE 1930S, WIDESPREAD automobile use generated a radical new form of theater design, one just as much a departure from traditional as the motel was from the hotel. Drive-in theaters, where the back of the projection screen usually doubled as a facade and an amorphous, if carefully graded, open space where the audience sat in cars served as the one-level auditorium, remained rare before World War II. With the return of peace, however, these places became standard highway fixtures across the country. Many were built on the edges of metropolitan areas, where they could be easily reached from new, outlying residential tracts and neighboring settlements of longstanding (pp. 194–195). Many other were erected just beyond sizable towns, where they could attract rural customers from a considerable radius as well as those from the host community (pp. 196–197). The appeal of the drive-in stemmed partly from the low price of admission, especially for cars full of family members or friends. Like the motel, they enabled a degree of privacy and, for young couples, intimacy unknown in conventional theaters. They provided a setting for people to show off their cars and enjoy some of the pleasures of being outside on summer evenings. An abundance of cheap land and comparatively low maintenance costs gave exhibitors financial reward even with low profit margins.

To create dramatic effects, the rear of the structure holding the projection screen was rendered as a giant piece of sculpture, suggestive, perhaps, of a world's fair building (pp. 198–199) or the ribs of a dam (p. 204). Elsewhere, this element was treated more like a giant billboard, its face proclaiming the establishment's name, enhanced by a few architectural (p. 205) or decorative (p. 200, top) features or even a painting (pp. 202–203). Entry and exit portals or flared wall screens that inhibited viewing by those who did not purchase tickets (p. 201, top) were frequently marshaled to further a sense of sculptural theatricality. Irrespective of means, drive-in owners sought to make a memorable impression among passing motorists. Sidney Lust, who owned a chain of drive-ins around Washington, D. C., embellished one of them with elements evocative of a classical public building (pp. 206–207), while in rural Missouri the Star's screen, its structure almost fully exposed, appears to be rising from a barn (p. 200, bottom). In cases where topography worked against placing the screen parallel to the road or where owners wished to place the facility further from moving traffic, portals were the primary means to eliciting attention (p. 201, bottom). In some later examples with more than a single screen and the staging area set well back from ever more expensive highway frontage, a vivacious portal treatment was essential to demarking the theater's presence (opposite).

Many other forms of entertainment sprouted up along the highway as well. Kiddie parks, miniature golf courses and driving ranges, menageries, privately exhibited natural wonders such as caves and chasms, bowling alleys, roller rinks, and bars were among the places of diversion catering to audiences of varying ages. Souvenir shops, antique stores, fruit and/or vegetable stands, handmade furniture outlets, salvage yards, fireworks sheds, and other specialized places for sale and sometimes trade along the highway might also be considered places of entertainment as they were generally patronized by people during their

leisure time. I confess I failed to photograph most such places during the 1970s simply because they did not then interest me as much as the types illustrated in this volume. Occasionally, a building's design was so unusual, such as the Dreamland dance hall near Huntington, West Virginia, it was to me irresistible (pp. 6–7). But a facility far more typical of many such places—inexpensive and unpretentious—was a dance hall outside Columbus, Ohio, which was one of the first photographs of roadside architecture I ever took—not I fear for documentary reasons, but because its proprietor was some unknown and long-lost relative (p. 208). In was an inauspicious beginning for what soon became a passion.

*Harrisonburg Drive In Theatre, U. S. Route 11, Harrisonburg, Virginia (July 1972)*

*Sky-Vu Drive-In Theatre, U. S. Route 40, Russell, Kansas (October 1977)*
FOLLOWING PAGES: *Ridge Pike Drive-In Theatre, 1949, Ridge Pike, Norristown, Pennsylvania (May 1970)*

*Sunset Drive-In Theatre, Amarillo, Texas (November 1972)*

*Star Drive-In Theatre, U. S. Route 65, Marshall, Missouri (July 197.*

*Cactus Drive-In Theatre, Albuquerque, New Mexico (November 1972)*

*Saratoga Drive-In Theatre, near Albany, New York (August 1971)*
FOLLOWING PAGES: *Sunset Drive-In Theatre, Independence, Kansas (October 1979)*

*Melody Drive-In Theatre, U. S. Route 40, east of Springfield, Ohio (February 1971)*

*Midway Drive In Theatre, U.S. Route 20, North Kingsville, Ohio (October 1972)*
FOLLOWING PAGES: *Sidney Lust's Drive-In Theatre, 1947, U.S. Route 1, Beltsville, Maryland (April 1971);*

# A Note on the Photographs

*Al Longstreth's Dancing, U. S. Route 40, west of Columbus, Ohio (August 1968)*

**EXCEPT FOR THE VERY** earliest images in this book, all photographs were taken with a Nikon F 35mm camera using a Nikon 35mm, perspective control lens or, in a few cases, a Nikon 105mm lens. I used Kodachrome II (later Kodachrome 25) color slide film exclusively, save for rare instances where I could not procure it.

The figures are identified based on my notes taken at the time of visit, with the month and year noted in parentheses. In some cases, I have added information that I found in later years. I have made no attempt to indicate the current state of the buildings or whether they remain extant.